grade 6

COMMON
PLACE
— *book* —

Identity & Gift

We are invited on a journey—a journey of discovery and wonder. In *Man and Woman He Created Them: A Theology of the Body*, Pope St. John Paul II brings us back to Scripture to rediscover who we are and the greatness to which we are called.

To help you along the journey, you have your own Theology of the Body Commonplace Book. Inside you will find lessons, discussion questions and spaces for you to write, draw, question, record and make connections.

What is a "commonplace book"? It's different than a diary, or even a reading journal. It is a "common place" to hold ideas, thoughts, copy inspirational quotes and, in some cases, for drawing and artwork. The process of copying and writing by hand slows you down and lets you think more carefully and deeply about things that interest you. Below is a list of many famous writers, inventors and world leaders who have used commonplace books:

- Marcus Aurelius
- Mark Twain
- Alexis de Tocqueville
- Charles Dickens
- Henry D. Thoreau
- Thomas Jefferson

- Isaac Newton
- Thomas Edison
- Leonardo da Vinci
- E.M. Forster
- Marie Curie

UNIT ONE:

CREATION IS A
gift

Reflect on your *lectio divina* time. What is a phrase or image that stands out to you? Write or draw below.

Record a verse to memorize.

"FOR THOU DIDST FORM MY INWARD PARTS, THOU DIDST KNIT ME TOGETHER IN MY MOTHER'S WOMB."

-PSALM 139:13

"THE HEAVENS ARE TELLING THE GLORY OF GOD; AND THE FIRMAMENT PROCLAIMS HIS HANDIWORK."

Psalm 19:1

CREATION IS A GIFT

Pope St. John Paul II saw something special in the creation account of Genesis. He didn't see it only as the account of something that happened a long time ago. He saw in Genesis our story, the story of what it means to be human. As he read and meditated on the Word of God in Genesis, John Paul II began to see that this account of the very beginning of creation could

001

help us understand God, ourselves and the world in a deeper way. What exactly can we learn? That is what he wrote about in *Man and Woman He Created Them: A Theology of the Body*, which we will learn more about in the following units.

In the account of Genesis, God reveals himself as the Creator. He brings light into darkness. He creates stars, galaxies and planets. He puts dry land and sea where before there was nothing. He makes trees and vines and grasses and flowers spring up and be fruitful. He gives living creatures a beautiful, wild land to live in and explore. And to the human person, he gave a very special gift: the gift of being created in his image and likeness.

"God looked at everything he had made and found it very good" (Genesis 1:31). Why does God create this wild, wonderful and good world? God is already complete, so he didn't need the world—no one made him create it—but we know that God does create the world, so we know that he cares about the world. God cares about it so much that he loves the world into existence. The world is a gift from God—it is given entirely out of love. He wants to share and give life to others.

"THE WORLD IS A GIFT FROM GOD."

John Paul II says creation is a "gift" (TOB 13:3). What does this mean? We have first to think about what a gift is. Suppose when you woke up tomorrow morning there was a large box with a ribbon and your name on it sitting outside your bedroom door. How would you respond? Would you smile or cry? Would you be happy or worried? Would you sit down and open it right away or casually walk past and brush your teeth first? Most likely you would be surprised, excited and happy. You somehow know that a gift is something good, not harmful or scary. You would wonder who gave it to you, and you would be sure that it was someone who cared about you. Even if it turned out to be something you wouldn't have chosen, isn't it still special, perhaps even more so, than if you had chosen it yourself?

A gift is something that is given: there is one who gives and one who receives, and in giving and receiving a relationship is established between them. A gift usually brings with it some surprise (because it wasn't your idea), excitement (because it wasn't necessary, but was given anyway) and happiness. In addition, there is something about the gift that will always remind you of the one who gave it to you. For example, if your best friend gave you the gift, in keeping the gift, using it and having it around, you would feel close to your friend. The gift connects the one who gives to the one who receives.

> "IN RECEIVING THIS GIFT, WE ARE CONNECTED TO THE GIVER OF THE GIFT."

John Paul II has all of this in mind when he says that creation is a gift. We receive ourselves and all of creation as good, and therefore a gift. In receiving this gift, we are connected to the Giver of the gift. The gift from your friend will always remind you of who your friend is and your friendship with him or her. In a similar way, when we look at all of creation, we are reminded of who God is and of his plan for the world.

THE WORLD IS GOOD

By calling creation a gift, John Paul II communicates two important ideas. First, he points to God's motivation for creating a world in the first place.

Remember: God isn't forced to create the world, but because of who he is he generously and freely gives the gift of life. Second, God's giving is the ultimate gift because "the gift comes into being precisely from nothing" (TOB 13:3). For us, when we make and give a gift we always use materials that are already there (like paper, glue and string) and make something new (like an ornament). But God creates out of nothing (*ex nihilo*). He not only makes something new, he also creates and designs all the materials. It's difficult to think about this: there was nothing and now there is something.

The gift of our lives and all of creation is first and foremost that we exist. Our existence is the first gift. Think of it this way: before you do, say, think or give anything, you first must exist. If you don't exist, you can't do anything. All of creation, and in a special way the human person, is a gift first because it exists and God says, "It is good."

My life and all creation are the result of a generous, free gift because God is love (1 John 4:8). Think about that for a moment. What is your favorite animal? Your favorite place to play or hang out? Who is your best friend? Do you have siblings? Everything is given and meant to be received as a gift. How do we receive the gift well? We receive the gift well when we see it the way God sees it. In other words, when we treat each person, place and thing with the reverence and love it deserves.

> "MY LIFE AND ALL OF CREATION ARE GOOD . . . BECAUSE WE EXIST."

In Genesis when God creates the universe, he says again and again, "It is good." He doesn't say, "It is good because it does something." My life and all of creation are good not because we *do* something but simply because we exist. This fact cannot change no matter what happens to us in life.

God creates and fashions us, sees us and knows us. Even when other people ignore or misunderstand us, God stays with us. The truth is that his love in creating us doesn't stop at the first moment of our existence but is present at every moment of our lives. God is not just close to his creation, he is present within it. In other words, God's gift of creation is not just something that happened once a long time ago, and told to us in Genesis. It is something happening at every moment, as he gives the gift of life to his creatures. This means that no matter what difficulties or sufferings we face in this life, we are never alone. He is invisible but with us in everything. God has a plan for our future that not even death can prevent, for we are made for eternal life with him. It is good that we exist.

GOD'S IRREVERSIBLE LOVE

In creating the world, God reveals his goodness and love and his desire to share that with us. Nothing has happened, or ever will happen, to change that. Even when Adam and Eve sinned, God did not take back the gift of his love which was expressed in the creation of the world. Instead, he sent his Son, Jesus, into the world to save us from sin and to be a witness to the irreversible love of God.

003

This love sees us, knows us and cares for us, just because we *are*. He will never change his mind about us. The gift of creation and the gift of redemption remind us of that. This is the love God loves us with, and the kind of love we are called to give to others. In loving others, John Paul II writes, "[I] *become a gift* and—through this gift—[I] fulfill the very meaning" and purpose of my life (TOB 15:1). We receive ourselves as a gift and are called to give ourselves as a gift. Remaining in the love of God and sharing that love with others are the beginning of real and lasting happiness.

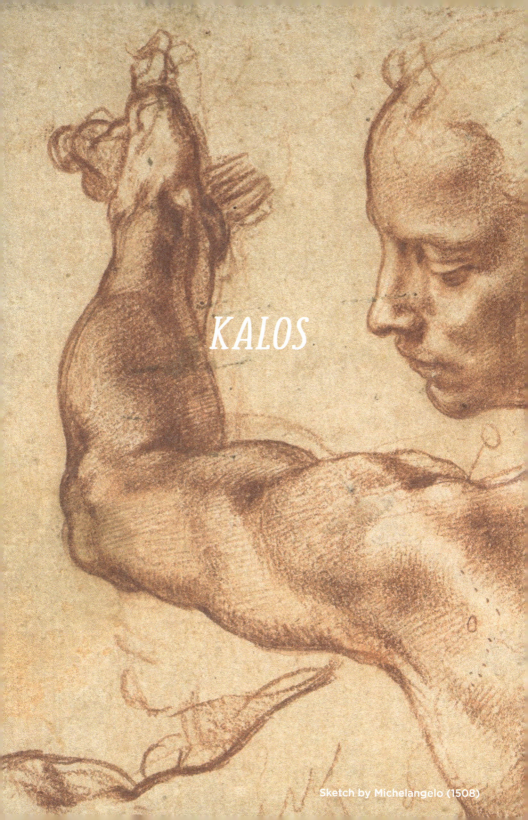

KALOS

1. List characteristics needed in order to call something a "gift".

2. Is something a gift if you are forced to hand it over? If it's not a gift, what is it?

3. Is something a gift if you have to give something else in exchange for it? If it's not a gift, what is it?

4. If you gave someone a gift and he didn't say "thank you", or he didn't seem excited about it, would this bother you? Why or why not?

5. Reflect on your experience: What does it mean to receive a gift well? List characteristics or reactions you'd like to see when you give a gift.

6. Reflect on your experience: Think about an experience you had in either receiving or giving a gift. What does the gift say about the giver and the receiver? Who determines the meaning of the gift? Is there something of the giver contained in the gift?

"EVERY CREATURE BEARS WITHIN ITSELF THE SIGN OF THE ORIGINAL AND FUNDAMENTAL GIFT."

–TOB 13:4

EXPERIENCE

Sketch by Michelangelo (1508)

Name: Blessed Pier Giorgio Frassati
Feast Day: July 4

Pier Giorgio was born in Turin, Italy in 1901. From a young age, he had a deep love for God and neighbor, as well as a special devotion to the Eucharist. Pier Giorgio was an outstanding witness to the joy and generosity of Christ. He was involved in many societies and organizations for Catholic youth and spread the message of the Gospel through his words and deeds. His generosity to the poor was extravagant, and he was even known to walk many miles because he had given the last of his bus money away. In addition, he spent many hours serving the needs of the poor and sick of Turin.

004

Pier Giorgio was very active, and could often be found mountain climbing or skiing. Often heading into the mountains with friends, he saw God's beauty and glory in all that was created. The gift and goodness of creation were clear to him. In his enjoyment of creation, he was brought closer to the Creator. Pier Giorgio contracted polio and died at the young age of 24. At his beatification in 1990, John Paul II called him "The Man of the Eight Beatitudes" for the way in which he lived the Gospel in everything he did. John Paul II said when visiting Pier Giorgio's tomb: "I wanted to pay homage to a young man who was able to witness to Christ. . . . When I was a young man, I, too, felt the beneficial influence of his example and, as a student, I was impressed by the force of his testimony."

Think of another saint or a hero from your own life. Is there a teacher, family member or friend who reminds you of Blessed Pier Giorgio Frassati?

Name: _____

Record 3 things you are grateful for *today*.

1) _____

   _____

2) _____

   _____

3) _____

   _____

Sketch something beautiful you saw or record an interesting quote you heard/read *today*.

CHALLENGE: Think of 3 different things *every day* for which you are grateful.

SUNDAY

1) _____
2) _____
3) _____

MONDAY

1) _____
2) _____
3) _____

TUESDAY

1) _____
2) _____
3) _____

WEDNESDAY

1) _____
2) _____
3) _____

THURSDAY

1) _____
2) _____
3) _____

FRIDAY

1) _____
2) _____
3) _____

SATURDAY

1) _____
2) _____
3) _____

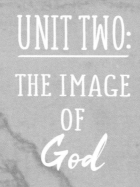

UNIT TWO:

THE IMAGE OF *God*

Sketch by Michelangelo (1508)

Reflect on your *lectio divina* time. What is a phrase or image that stands out to you? Write or draw below.

Record a verse to memorize.

"ARE NOT FIVE SPARROWS SOLD FOR TWO PENNIES? AND NOT ONE OF THEM IS FORGOTTEN BEFORE GOD. WHY, EVEN THE HAIRS OF YOUR HEAD ARE ALL NUMBERED. FEAR NOT; YOU ARE OF MORE VALUE THAN MANY SPARROWS."

–LUKE 12:6–7

"GOD CREATED MANKIND IN HIS IMAGE; IN THE IMAGE OF GOD HE CREATED THEM; MALE AND FEMALE HE CREATED THEM."

Genesis 1:27

PART OF CREATION, YET SET APART

Even though each human person is totally unique (there will never be another you), there are some things that everyone has in common. No matter what country you come from, what age you are or even what your personality type is, some things are the same for all of us simply because we are human. This is called human nature. Every creature bears within itself the mark of the generous and good Creator. And the human person, created male and female, bears this mark in the deepest way possible.

In Genesis chapter one, everything is created in a certain order: first the ground and the sky, then plants and trees, then most animals, then mammals and finally, the human person. John Paul II saw that while *all* creation is made good and holy ("and God saw that it was good"), it is also the case that with each progressive day of creation, each creature is made higher in status until finally we arrive at the human person. This lines up with our experience of the world and how we treat it.

For example, we would sit on a rock, but not on the vegetables in the garden. We walk on the ground, but not on our pet. I would walk my dog on a leash, but not my little brother. Why is that? As we go further up the chain of creation, we see creatures that are capable of being alive, of feeling, of willing, of thinking and of loving. In other words, you have creatures that are *more like God*. It is clear from the Genesis account that there is something very different about the creation of the human person. The rest of creation only bears traces or shadows of who God is, while the human person is made in the image and likeness of God. This doesn't mean that the rock or the vegetables or the chickens aren't special or good. They *are* good because God creates them and pronounces their goodness. This means they are given as a gift and therefore have their proper place in the world. As a gift, there is special honor and reverence that is due to all created things.

> ## "EACH CREATURE IS MADE IN HIGHER STATUS UNTIL WE FINALLY ARRIVE AT THE HUMAN PERSON."

IMAGE AND LIKENESS

The human person, created male and female, is most like God in all of material creation. What does this mean? Of course, when we talk about man being "like God," it's important to realize that we only say this by *analogy*. An analogy is a way of describing two things that are *similar* but also very *dissimilar*. For example, I could say, "He is as strong as an ox." There is something similar about the person and an ox: they are both strong. But there is also something different: my friend is not an ox, and in fact, even the way each is strong is different.

When we talk about God, since he is far greater than anything we can think or imagine, we must realize that whatever we say about God will never be enough to describe him exactly as he is. But there is an important similarity between the human person and God that he gives us by creating us in his "image and likeness." It is this similarity that sets the human person apart from the rest of creation, and allows him to be in a special relationship with God.

To be a human person means to be the kind of being that has the ability to think, to freely choose and to be in a special relationship with God himself. The human person is able to understand the meaning of the gift of creation, and be a "partner" with God in a covenantal way (TOB 6:2). Because of this, God gives the human dominion over himself and all creation.

This is not to say that animals do not experience anything like feeling, thinking or choosing. Certainly, there is *something like* these things happening in animals. For example, if your dog is chasing a squirrel but you call him away, there is something in him that must make a "choice" about what to do; he's not just a robot. But it's important to realize that the way animals experience these things is very different than the way humans do. Compare the example of calling your dog and calling your friend on the playground. If both your dog and friend heard you and decided to ignore you, would you have the same reaction? Likely you would be more upset with your friend than your dog, because we sense that the powers of feeling, thinking, choosing and even loving are different in persons and animals.

This does not mean that animals and other creatures are not important or can be used however I like; in fact, it is just the opposite! Because the human person is higher than the rest of creation, he is required to serve creation and help it flourish. The more authority someone has, the more responsibility to serve that person has as well. Because of man's special dignity and uniqueness, he alone can understand the meaning of the gift of creation. Therefore it is his responsibility to care for it and protect it. This is seen when Adam *names* the animals; when God calls man to have *dominion over* the earth; and when Adam is told to *till and keep* the earth.

IMAGE OF THE TRINITY

The human person is made in the image and likeness of God. Who is God? God has revealed himself to be the Creator who is a Trinity: Father, Son and Holy Spirit. We believe in one God who is three persons. God is love, a communion of persons. This means that the human person is made in the image and likeness of love. Man's whole life is made up of a web of relationships. Think about it for a moment: when did a person ever come into existence without anyone else? When has a person ever survived without another person, or without eating food or breathing air?

John Paul II says there are four basic relationships that every human person has from the very moment he begins to exist: his relationship to God, to himself, to others and to the world. We live, survive, love and are happy because of these important relationships. In fact, it is in relationship that we realize who we are. Each individual person is made in the image and likeness of God, but also man images God in these important relationships. John Paul II writes: "Man was created in the image of God inasmuch as he is male and female . . . Man became the image of God not only through his own humanity, but also through the communion of persons" (TOB 9:3).

008

We have seen the greatness of all creation as well as the special place of the human person. Being made in the image of God means that man has a fundamental dignity that can never be taken away. God is present to us, with us and in us, 24 hours a day, holding us in existence. God sees, knows, loves and wills each of us to exist and share in his life. He wants us to live, grow, discover and explore this good world he gave us and have eternal happiness.

"GOD IS LOVE, A COMMUNION OF PERSONS."

Even though I will always be in the image of God, my likeness to him can grow or wither based on the way I live my life. Being in the image of God is automatic and unchangeable, but I am called, through my actions, to live out that imaging and become more and more like God. This is begun in small daily tasks of charity and striving to live virtuously, always seeking the true good of others and myself. I am called to receive the world and my life as a gift. I am called to treat that gift with respect and care and help all creation become more of what it was created to be. I am called to love each and every human person and make my life a gift to them.

009

Notes by Alexander Graham Bell

KALOS

Music by Wolfgang Amadeus Mozart

1. What do we have in common with everything that is created? What makes humans different from the rest of creation?

_____

_____

_____

_____

_____

_____

_____

_____

_____

_____

_____

2. What in creation looks closest to us? What makes it similar to us? What looks most different?

_____

_____

_____

_____

_____

_____

_____

_____

_____

_____

_____

_____

3. To be made in the image of God means we are "like God". What are some specific ways we are like God? How are we not like God?

_____

_____

_____

_____

_____

_____

_____

_____

_____

_____

_____

_____

4. Why does man have a special responsibility to care for creation and preserve it, like Adam?

_____

_____

_____

_____

_____

_____

_____

_____

_____

_____

5. What are some ways in which you can show proper reverence and respect for all creation?

6. We learned that man has four basic relationships: to God, himself, others and the world. What do these basic relationships tell us about our lives and what we are called to do?

7. Make a list of things that are unique to the human person (for example, laughing or making artwork).

_____

_____

_____

_____

_____

_____

_____

_____

_____

_____

_____

_____

_____

"MAN IS THE IMAGE OF GOD NOT ONLY BY HIMSELF, BUT ALSO THROUGH THE COMMUNION OF PERSONS."
—TOB 9:3

EXPERIENCE

Music by Wolfgang Amadeus Mozart

Name: St. Teresa of Calcutta
Feast Day: September 5

010

Born in Albania in 1910, Agnes Bojaxhiu felt early on a call to religious life. She joined the Sisters of Loreto in Ireland in order to learn English and be formed as a missionary. Several years after her final profession, she experienced "a call within a call" to found a new community called the Missionaries of Charity, dedicated to helping the poorest of the poor, beginning in Calcutta, India. After receiving the blessing of her bishop and her religious superior, she began with a home for the dying, called a hospice. Gradually it grew to help all those who were in need. Mother Teresa spent the rest of her life ministering to the poor, the blind, the lame, the handicapped and even lepers. She and her sisters dedicated all of their lives to being with those most in need. No matter a person's circumstances, actions or sickness, she treated all with care and respect. Mother Teresa was committed to upholding the dignity of every human person from conception to death and loving everyone as God loves them.

In 1979 she won the Nobel Peace Prize for her humanitarian work, and she reminded us that true social justice is concerned with the whole person, stating that the greatest poverty of all is the absence of love. Now there are hundreds of Missionaries of Charity throughout the world carrying on this mission. At her beatification, John Paul II said of her: "I am personally grateful to this courageous woman whom I have always felt beside me. Mother Teresa, an icon of the Good Samaritan, went everywhere to serve Christ in the poorest of the poor. Not even conflict and war could stand in her way. . . . Her greatness lies in her ability to give without counting the cost, to give 'until it hurts'. Her life was a radical living and a bold proclamation of the Gospel." She was canonized in 2016.

Think of another saint or a hero from your own life. Is there a teacher, family member or friend who reminds you of St. Teresa of Calcutta?

Name: _____

Find new, little-known or unusual facts, pictures or articles about nature that you believe will amaze your classmates. Record your findings below and print out a picture to share with the class.

UNIT THREE:

THE
body
REVEALS
MAN

Reflect on your *lectio divina* time. What is a phrase or image that stands out to you? Write or draw below.

Record a verse to memorize.

"FOR WE ARE HIS WORKMANSHIP, CREATED IN CHRIST JESUS FOR GOOD WORKS."

–EPHESIANS 2:10A

> "DO YOU NOT KNOW THAT YOUR BODY IS A TEMPLE OF THE HOLY SPIRIT? . . .
> SO GLORIFY GOD IN YOUR BODY."
>
> 1 Corinthians 6:19–20

THE BODY: WITNESS TO CREATION AS GIFT

The human person, made in the image and likeness of God, is part of the created world. Yet he is also set apart from all of creation because of his unique and special relationship with God. In this special relationship, God gives the whole world to man as a gift and invites man to help care for all that has been made. John Paul II notes that by walking and living among the other creatures

O11

of this world, man realizes he is different. He looks around and notices that his body is different than all the other kinds of creatures. Why is this important? We "look different" than other things—why is that a big deal? John Paul II helps us answer these questions. Adam and Eve first realize their special place in creation through their bodies, and by seeing the special meaning of the body, they are able to understand themselves and the rest of creation more clearly.

We can understand more about ourselves through the body. As John Paul II writes: "The body reveals man" (TOB 9:4). Let's think about that. Look around the room. How many people are in the room? How do you know that? You probably started by counting how many people you see in the room. You can only see them because they have bodies, and because you have a body with which to see or notice them. The body makes us aware of the presence of another human person. It reveals who and what is there—the body reveals the person: it is not a container holding the real person on the inside. The "human being, created 'in

> "I DID NOT
> CREATE MYSELF:
> I COME FROM
> ANOTHER."

012

the image of God' (Genesis 1:27), 'is a body'" (TOB 8:1). In other words, your body helps to express who you really are.

What can the human body remind me of? It reminds me that I did not create myself: I come from another. I have been given to myself. My life is a gift, and it is good I exist. I have received myself and my life as a gift, and I am called to take part in that gift giving by making a gift of myself to others. My body also reminds me that I am made for relationship.

Everything about the structure of my body shows that I am a being made to be in relationship with the world, which includes everything from the ground I walk on to the people that surround me. Even the most basic bodily functions, like breathing air and eating food, remind me that I am a relational being. I need these things in order to survive. Without these things, I can't exist. Being born into a family and my biological connections to others also remind me that I did not create myself and that I am made to depend on and belong to the world in a special way. My body reminds me of who I am and shows me that all of creation is a gift.

THE HUMAN PERSON: BODY AND SOUL

Let's take a closer look at what it means that the body reveals man. Like all of creation, man is visible and material. If you were asked to describe your friend, you might state his height, describe his hair and eye color and list other physical features.

> "BODY AND SOUL ARE IN EACH OTHER AND WORK SIMULTANEOUSLY."

These are what we consider the *visible* parts of a person. Certainly, this is part of what makes him who he is, but these would not be the only things you would use to describe him. This is because the human person also has another dimension that is *invisible*, not material. This is what we call soul. But these are not two parts that make one whole. It's not an equation: body + soul = human person. Rather, the visible body and the invisible soul are always deeply united.

In other words, both body and soul are in each other and work simultaneously, all the time. Think about it: can you do anything with just your body or just your soul? Even when you raise your hand to ask a question, it is your soul that allows you to do that. When you think or pray, that is only possible because you have a body and organs that help make the thought and prayer happen. Instead of thinking of the person as body + soul, it's better to think of a living body or an embodied soul.

Even though the body and soul work together all the time, there is a hierarchy, or order, between them. John Paul II, with the Church, says that "the 'invisible' determines man more than the 'visible'" (TOB 7:4). What does this mean? While both body and soul are essential to the human person and each are deeply united, the hierarchy between them

means that the soul is higher than the body. This is because the soul cannot be corrupted or be broken down like the body. Or think of the description of your friend. Though his height, hair color, etc. are all truly part of him, you have an intuition that there is something more than what is visible, and that what is invisible has more weight, so to speak.

To say this in no way means the body is lesser or not important, but quite the opposite. Our bodies are not just for this lifetime. Sin introduced death and corruption into the world, and we see this in a very clear way in our bodies. We only get sick and old and die because of sin. It wasn't supposed to be that way when God created man. However, the Church teaches that, even though we die, at the end of time we will get our bodies back in a new way, and they will no longer be corruptible. They will never age or get sick again. The body is made to be immortal, though as a result of sin, it must die first.

Let's look at an example to help us see the unity and hierarchy of body and soul. Suppose one of your classmates comes up to you and kicks you in the shins. Later at lunch, you relate the story to your friends. How would you explain it? Likely you would say something like: "Can you believe it?! He just came up to me and kicked me for no reason." Notice—you wouldn't say "he kicked my body" but rather "he kicked *me*." You could say "he kicked my body," but somehow it fails to capture what was done to you. It was *you* that was hurt, and the hurt your classmate caused is more than the pain in your leg.

We identify with our bodies. Anything that happens to your body happens to you. In other words, you could never go up to someone, punch them in the face and say, "Oh no, that wasn't personal! I was just doing that to your body, but not to you!" There is another layer to this. Even though we want to say, "I am my body," it's just as important to add, "I am more than my body." We can't only be our bodies. Remember the hurt from being kicked in the leg? It wasn't only the physical pain, it was also something much deeper than that. Just as I identify with my body, I also have a gut feeling that I surpass my body, that there is something more to who I am. For no matter what happens to my body (losing an arm or leg, getting sick, etc.), I am still fully human with unchangeable dignity. The important point here is that both things are true: I am my body, even as I am more than my body.

"GLORIFY GOD IN YOUR BODY" (1 CORINTHIANS 6:20)

014

All that we have said about the body helps us to understand more clearly who we are, and reminds us not to take the body for granted. The body is not something I have with which I can do whatever I want. The body is full of meaning. We can say that the body is able to speak without words. What does it say? The body is a witness to our being as gift, a sign of Divine love in the world (TOB 19:4). Being a sign of Divine love and communion in this world also holds within it a challenge to discover how I can be a stronger and stronger sign of it. I am not only meant to receive myself as a gift, but I am meant to give myself as a gift and live more deeply the image of God within me.

Because our body-soul unity is so real, St. Paul calls the body a "temple," a holy place of revelation, and why we can "glorify God in [our] body" (1 Cor 6:19–20). Because we are embodied, our bodies are important for how we relate to God in prayer. We are meant to relate to God with our whole selves, as embodied souls. We see this in a special way in the sacraments and when we participate in liturgy. We stand, sit, kneel, make the sign of the cross, sing, burn incense, light candles and surround ourselves with beautiful and holy images. God himself confirms the importance of the body when he saves us from sin by becoming flesh (taking on a body), dying and rising again (TOB 23:4).

"THE BODY IS FULL OF MEANING."

KALOS

Ornamental Page from Greek Gospels (date unknown)

1. Does your body communicate even without saying anything with words? How so?

2. How might I be able to tell when someone is angry even if he or she hasn't told me so? How about sad, defeated or happy?

3. How do you know when you're sick? What evidence do you have or feel to show that you have a cold or the flu, etc.?

4. How does the body reveal the person? What is different about the human body compared to any other animal or plant body?

5. What does it mean to say "I am my body, even though I am more than my body"?

6. If my life is a gift, do I decide the meaning of the gift? Is it enough to say simply "It's my body; I can do whatever I want with it"? Why or why not? What more would you want to say about that?

_____

_____

_____

_____

_____

_____

_____

_____

_____

_____

_____

_____

_____

_____

_____

_____

"THE 'INVISIBLE' DETERMINES MAN MORE THAN THE 'VISIBLE.'"
—TOB 7:4

EXPERIENCE

Ornamental Page from Greek Gospels (date unknown)

Name: St. André Bessette
Feast Day: January 6

André Bessette was born in Canada in 1845. At age 12, both his parents died and he went to live with a new family. Growing up he tried his hand at many different jobs without success. Rather than be discouraged, André worked simply and joyfully at whatever work he could find. Feeling the call to religious life, he joined the Congregation of the Holy Cross. Because of his weak health, his entrance was delayed. When he finally entered, he was given the humble job of doorkeeper at Notre Dame College in Montréal, since he lacked the skills or knowledge for other roles in the community.

015

Brother André had a great devotion to St. Joseph and spent many long nights in prayer in his room near the door of the monastery. He often visited the sick, and through the intercession of St. Joseph, many were cured of their illnesses when he prayed for them. His presence and attention were a comfort to many, and he became known as a great friend to all in need. Soon hundreds of people were coming to see the lowly doorkeeper to ask for prayers and healing of soul and body. Though in the eyes of the world Brother André did not seem to accomplish much, he brought God's healing to many. He also helped found an oratory in honor of St. Joseph, where many people today still travel to ask for St. André's intercession. Hundreds of miracles have occurred, showing the great power of God to work through this simple and holy man. He was canonized in 2010.

Think of another saint or a hero from your own life. Is there a teacher, family member or friend who reminds you of St. André Bessette?

Name:

Questions for future class sessions:

Sketch by Thomas Edison

Bring your questions to God: write and pray.

_____
_____
_____
_____
_____
_____
_____
_____
_____
_____

"FOR FROM HIM AND THROUGH HIM
AND TO HIM ARE ALL THINGS."

–ROMANS 11:36

Write any personal resolutions you are inspired to record.

_____

_____

_____

_____

_____

_____

_____

_____

_____

_____

_____

_____

_____

_____

UNIT FOUR:

ORIGINAL
solitude

Reflect on your *lectio divina* time. What is a phrase or image that stands out to you? Write or draw below.

Record a verse to memorize.

"BE STRONG AND OF GOOD COURAGE, DO NOT FEAR OR BE IN DREAD OF THEM: FOR IT IS THE LORD YOUR GOD WHO GOES WITH YOU; HE WILL NOT FAIL YOU OR FORSAKE YOU."

–DEUTERONOMY 31:6

"[T]HEN THE LORD GOD FORMED THE MAN OUT OF DUST FROM THE GROUND AND BLEW INTO HIS NOSTRILS THE BREATH OF LIFE, AND THE MAN BECAME A LIVING BEING."

Genesis 2:7

THE ORIGINAL EXPERIENCES

Though God is present in all of creation, he also wishes to communicate and share his life in a special way with the human person. This is because man is made in the image and likeness of God. "Revelation" is the word we use to talk about God making himself known in a clear and direct way. How does he do this? Does he come out of the sky and speak in a way our ears can hear? It is true that sometimes God reveals himself in this way, but what we mean by revelation is the way he speaks in Sacred Scripture and the Holy Tradition of the Church. This revelation, always present in some form from the beginning, was confirmed in the Old Covenant of Israel, fulfilled in Christ, and has been entrusted to the Church today. Revelation helps us to know what is most true about the human person and helps us to make more sense of life.

Revelation is not disconnected from who we are, nor is it simply God's Word coming from on high telling us what to do. Rather, revelation has a deep connection to the human heart and helps us to understand what it is we desire more than anything else. Therefore John Paul II also believed that reflecting on our own experience along with revelation can be a helpful guide to answering the important questions of our lives. God has placed deep within the human

"REVELATION HELPS US TO KNOW WHAT IS MOST TRUE ABOUT THE HUMAN PERSON."

heart a desire for truth, goodness and beauty. His Word to us affirms something deep within our souls. God sees and understands us. He knows who we are and what we desire, even better than we understand ourselves. His Word, given to us, helps us to be more fully alive.

"Experience" doesn't just mean "how I personally see the world," but rather, "how I see the world in the light of truth." For example, if you went on a field trip with your class to the zoo, you each would have your own personal experience of what the trip was like. On the bus ride home, you might tell each other about the animals you saw, which were your favorite, and maybe even something you saw that nobody else did. You each had your own "experience" of the day, but that's not all experience is.

What if one of your friends came on the bus and started talking about the microwaves, rocket ships and refrigerators in the cages at the zoo? Is that the truth about what is in the cages? Would you describe that as a true experience or a false impression? Do you see how, even though everyone's "experience" of the zoo is different, it isn't so different that it escapes the truth of what is in reality? John Paul II taught that the truth about reality is the anchor for being able to trust our own unique vision of the world. This is what he means when he refers to "experience."

> "THESE 'ORIGINAL EXPERIENCES' REVEAL WHO WE ARE AT THE DEEPEST LEVEL."

In the creation of man, John Paul II saw and named three "original experiences": original solitude, original unity and original nakedness. These experiences are called "original" because they are experiences of our original parents, Adam and Eve. In this way they are original in the sense of happening "first", but they are also called "original" because they are the experiences common to all of us. They are called original because they are "foundational" to what it means to be human.

Though we all have many experiences in our lives, these "original experiences" reveal who we are at the deepest level, and therefore are the experiences on which every other human experience is based. Once again, we see that the account of Genesis is not simply the retelling of something that happened a long time ago but is also telling us about what it means to be human *now*. In a way, the experiences of Adam and Eve can teach us and shed light on who we are today.

SOLITUDE: ALONE–WITH–GOD

"IT IS IN THIS SOLITUDE THAT MAN REALIZES HIS UNIQUENESS."

The first of the original experiences is original solitude. After the creation of Adam, Genesis 2 recounts: "Then the Lord God said, 'It is not good that the man should be alone; I will make him a helper fit for him.' So out of the ground the Lord God formed every beast of the field and every bird of the air, and brought them to the man to see what he would call them; and whatever the man called every living creature, that was its name. The man gave names to all cattle, and to the birds of the air, and to every beast of the field; but for the man there was not found a helper fit for him."

Here we see that Adam experiences solitude. In some way, he stands alone when he looks around at all of creation. He is the only one of his kind, and he cannot find one "fit for him." John Paul II points out that this has two meanings. First, Adam's original solitude describes the difference between man and the rest of creation because he alone is in the image of God. Second, despite being surrounded by the rest of creation, Adam doesn't have another like him, which both Adam and God seem to think is "not good". Man (meaning humanity) is incomplete without both male and female.

But the meaning of original solitude isn't only negative, nor does it mean that Adam is isolated. Rather, his alone-ness points to the fact that, in all of creation, he alone is able to be in a deep and personal relationship with the Creator. In other words, Adam is alone, but *alone-with-God*. It is in this solitude that man realizes his uniqueness and understands what makes him special. So, while it is "not good" that man is alone, solitude makes him realize things about himself that he couldn't have learned otherwise.

Made in the image and likeness of God, man has knowledge and can understand, think, feel, choose and love in a way the rest of creation cannot. This uniqueness makes man able to have a special relationship with God: "Man is 'alone': this is to say that through his own humanity. . . [he is] at the same time set into a unique, exclusive, and unrepeatable relationship with God himself" (TOB 6:2). While original solitude does highlight man's alone-ness, John Paul II wants us to understand how it more importantly describes man's relationship to God.

REVEALED BY THE BODY

It is Adam's experience of his body that helps him become aware of his solitude and all that it means. Man is part of creation, and yet also set apart. On the one hand, man's body is what makes him similar to other visible, material creation. On the other hand, it's also what makes him different, for his body doesn't look like the bodies of the other creatures.

The difference in the structure of the human body allows man to work at specifically human activities. For example, Adam alone cultivates the land and uses it for his own purposes. "In this activity, the body expresses the person" (TOB 7:2). As we have seen, the body is not meaningless stuff, but rather, because of the unity of body and soul, the body is able to reveal man's special dignity. The body helps Adam realize who he is, in whose image he is made, and his special role in creation.

Original solitude was first experienced by Adam, but it is the experience of every human person. Even though we experience it differently than Adam, the main elements remain the same. As humans we experience ourselves as different than other species of plants, animals and other creatures. There are certain characteristics of being human that bind us all into one category. This is discovered first of all in and through the body, which has the power to express who I am as a person. My deepest identity as a person is that I am made in the image and likeness of God and am made for communion with him. My experience of original solitude means that I have a unique and unrepeatable relationship with God that cannot be erased or filled by any other kind of relationship. As St. Augustine once wrote: "You have made us for yourself, Lord, and our hearts are restless until they rest in you."

"THE BODY IS ABLE TO REVEAL MAN'S SPECIAL DIGNITY."

Letter written by Pope St. John Paul II

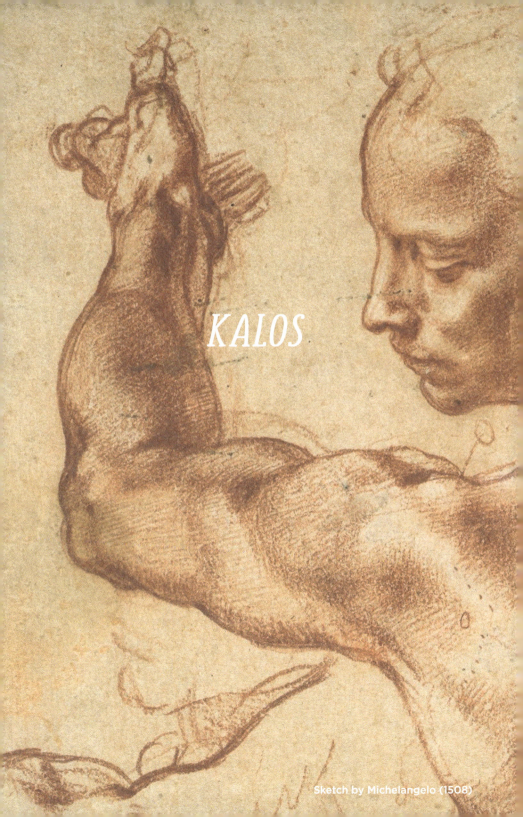

KALOS

Sketch by Michelangelo (1508)

1. Look back in your Commonplace Book (pages 74–76) on the meaning of "experience." Re-read the paragraph and example with your small group. Practice explaining it to each other. Why is it important not to think of experience as only "how I personally see the world"?

2. Think of a famous singer/songwriter whose music is really popular. When he wrote his music, was he writing about his own experiences or about experiences that are basic to all of us? Don't we have to say it's both? How is this similar and different than the original experiences?

3. What does "original solitude" mean? How is it both a positive and negative experience? How does Adam know he is "alone"?

4. Look around the room. Make a list of 10 things you see. How does the physical appearance of those items help you tell the difference between them? Is there something in the room that you don't recognize or cannot name? How will you find out what it is? How is this exercise similar to and different than Adam's experience of discovering the world?

5. Name some ways you can grow in your relationship to God, not just in the sacraments and other forms of prayer, but also in the way we love others and care for the gift of the world.

"MAN IS ALONE BECAUSE HE IS 'DIFFERENT' FROM THE VISIBLE WORLD . . . [HE HAS] A UNIQUE, EXCLUSIVE, AND UNREPEATABLE RELATIONSHIP WITH GOD HIMSELF."

–TOB 5:6–6:2

EXPERIENCE

Sketch by Michelangelo (1508)

Name: St. Mary of Egypt
Feast Day: April 2

Mary of Egypt was a holy and wise woman who lived as a hermit in the desert near the Holy Land. But her life was not always like that. She was born in 344 AD and at a young age left home and moved to the city of Alexandria where she quickly fell into a life of sin and dishonor. In search of further adventures she followed a group of pilgrims on their way to Jerusalem. As the account goes, Mary experienced a powerful conversion through an icon of the Blessed Mother in Jerusalem. Mary felt the call to a life of penance and solitude, alone with God in the desert across the Jordan River. For the next forty-seven years she lived a simple life of prayer and penance and grew in spiritual wisdom and virtue.

An account of Mary of Egypt was given by a priest traveling through the desert who brought her holy communion. He was impressed with her deep love of God, and after her death spread the news of this holy woman. Mary had a particular call to spend her life as a hermit, alone with God. This way of life reminds us all that no matter to what vocation we are called, the most fundamental and important relationship in our lives is with God. It also reminds us that even though Mary lived as a hermit, she was still connected to others in the Church in a spiritual and mystical way; her prayer and penance was offered up for herself and also for the life of the world.

Think of another saint or a hero from your own life. Is there a teacher, family member or friend who reminds you of St. Mary of Egypt?

Name:

Pick a slip of paper from the Gift-of-Self Box. Record your prayer, sacrifice or challenge below to help you remember it.

UNIT FIVE:

ORIGINAL
unity

Reflect on your *lectio divina* time. What is a phrase or image that stands out to you? Write or draw below.

Record a verse to memorize.

"IRON SHARPENS IRON, AND ONE MAN SHARPENS ANOTHER."

–PROVERBS 27:17

> **"THEN THE LORD GOD SAID: IT IS NOT GOOD FOR THE MAN TO BE ALONE.**
> **I WILL MAKE HIM A HELPER SUITED TO HIM."**
>
> Genesis 2:18

"NOT GOOD" THAT MAN BE ALONE

"The Lord God said: It is not good for the man to be alone. I will make a helper suited to him. So the Lord God formed out of the ground all the wild animals and all the birds of the air, and he brought them to the man to see what he would call them; whatever the man called each living creature was then its name. The man gave names to all the tame animals, all the birds of the air, and all the wild animals; but none proved to be a helper suited to the man" (Genesis 2:18–20).

For the first time in the creation account, God calls something "not good." God is speaking about something that is a key part of what it means to be human: we are not meant to be alone.

"WE ARE NOT MEANT TO BE ALONE."

It is true, as we learned before, that Adam's solitude has a positive meaning. Adam's solitude allows him to understand his own dignity as a person, his special relationship to God, and the greatness to which he is called by being the only one of his kind. And yet there is still something needed in order for Adam to better understand himself. He needs another "like himself," a "helper suited to him."

TWO WAYS OF BEING HUMAN: THE SAME AND DIFFERENT

"So the Lord God cast a deep sleep on the man, and while he was asleep, he took out one of his ribs and closed up its place with flesh. The Lord God then built the rib that he had taken from the man into

a woman. When he brought her to the man, the man said: 'This one, at last, is bone of my bones and flesh of my flesh; This one shall be called "woman," for out of man this one has been taken'" (Genesis 2:21–23).

Adam discovers in the creation of Eve one who is like himself, who shares the same human nature. Eve also experiences the original solitude that Adam does, thus, both Adam and Eve experience that they are different from the rest of the world. One of the ways this is immediately noticeable is in the structure of the body. When Adam sees Eve he exclaims, "This at last is bone of my bone and flesh of my flesh" (Genesis 2:23). It is the appearance of Eve as an embodied soul that gives Adam the first clue that she is human just as he is. He can recognize her as human because of her flesh and bones, and he realizes that this flesh and bone points to her deep spiritual reality, which he also shares. The body reveals the person. Their shared humanity shows the deep unity between them. In sharing the same nature, they also share the same dignity as human persons made in the image and likeness of God.

This unity does not mean that they are identical; there is an essential difference between Adam and Eve. Even though Adam and Eve share the same nature, they are not exactly the same in every way. Eve appears as human, but as a different kind of human than Adam. She is female, while Adam is male. In these two ways of being human man discovers more deeply who he is and how he is meant to relate to others and the world.

> "TO HAVE THE 'COMPLETE' PICTURE OF HUMANITY, YOU NEED TO SEE BOTH MALE AND FEMALE."

Adam, in seeing that there is another way to be human, realizes that he doesn't contain in himself all of what it means to be human. In other words, to have the "complete" picture of humanity, you need to see both male and female. Each has something that the other doesn't have. This is of course shown in the difference of bodies, but that difference of bodies goes much deeper and reveals a difference in how each relates to the world.

> ## "DIFFERENCE OF BODIES ... REVEALS A DIFFERENCE IN HOW EACH RELATES TO THE WORLD."

This is the meaning of original unity: the *unity-in-difference* of man and woman. In the creation of Eve, Adam now has one like himself that shares the same human nature (*unity*) and yet she is also different from him (*difference*). Their bodies reveal that they share the same nature, but they are different as male and female. Both things are true: men and women are the same but in different ways.

Male and female are two ways of being human. In this way, the human being especially mirrors God. God is a Trinity, Father, Son and Holy Spirit, three distinct persons who are one in substance; there is only one God (*unity*), but within that unity, there are three persons (*difference*). John Paul II writes that each person by him- or herself is in the image of God, but man is also in the image of God in this unity, or communion, of persons. Being in a communion of persons is something we already have experienced just by being born. It also speaks about the call of man to live for and with others. My life is a gift, and I am called to give myself as a gift to others and to the world.

MALE AND FEMALE: DIFFERENCE AS GOOD

John Paul II points out that there is something like joy in the exclamation of Adam when he sees Eve for the first time. He is rejoicing that he is no longer alone, and that there is another like him to share in his experience of the world. Even more, Adam takes delight in the difference between he and Eve. Why is the difference between Adam and Eve a good thing? Each of them can help the other understand himself more clearly and do things that couldn't be done if they are alone. The difference between Adam and Eve, male and female, is good.

022

John Paul II points out that according to the original Hebrew text, the word that referred to Adam before the creation of Eve was a term used to describe humanity in general ('adam). After the creation of Eve, when Adam awakens from sleep, the word used in Scripture to refer to Adam is different ('is) and corresponds to the word for the woman ('issa). Why does John Paul II bring this up? He thinks this shows one of the reasons that the difference between man and woman is good. Adam really only

understands himself more fully when he sees another who is the same-and-different, namely, the woman. This is shown in the change of name: 'adam to 'is.

In the same way, Eve understands herself more fully when faced with the man. The difference between the two confirms the identity of each and helps each see what makes him or -herself unique. Both Adam and Eve gain a better understanding of themselves when faced with the difference of the other. Both see what they have, what the other has differently, and how the two can work together.

"THE DIFFERENCE BETWEEN MAN AND WOMAN IS GOOD."

Sometimes it is only by seeing what is different from us that we realize what makes us unique. For example, have you ever traveled somewhere far away where the people speak differently, dress differently, or even eat different foods? Did the experience of something different help you see more clearly what makes where you come from special? The difference is good because it helps us understand ourselves more and also shows us that there is more than one way to live and be in the world. While this is only an analogy, there is something similar going on when John Paul II reflects on man's experience of original unity. The human person as male and female make up a unity-in-difference that reflects who God is and reminds us of who we are and what we are called to do.

Notes written by Alexander Graham Bell

KALOS

Music by Wolfgang Amadeus Mozart

1. What does "original unity" mean? Why was it important for Adam to have another "like himself"? How does he recognize Eve as one "like himself"?

_____

_____

_____

_____

_____

_____

_____

_____

_____

_____

_____

_____

_____

_____

_____

_____

_____

_____

2. Did you ever face a big task or a chore that was made easier when someone came to help you with it? Did you feel relieved, frustrated, happy, annoyed, etc.? Why/why not?

_____

_____

_____

_____

_____

_____

3. Reflect on the same scenario from Question #2, but with a different twist: Perhaps you didn't need help to do a task or chore on your own, but was it more enjoyable when someone did it with you "just because"? Why/why not?

4. Think of your best friend. Why are you friends? What do you have in common? How are you different? Are the differences positive or negative?

_____

_____

_____

_____

_____

_____

_____

_____

_____

_____

_____

_____

_____

_____

5. Do you think you would like to be friends with someone who was exactly like you in every way? Why/why not?

_____

_____

_____

_____

_____

_____

_____

_____

_____

_____

_____

_____

_____

_____

_____

_____

"MASCULINITY AND FEMININITY [ARE] . . . TWO RECIPROCALLY COMPLETING WAYS OF 'BEING A BODY' AND AT THE SAME TIME OF BEING HUMAN."

—TOB 10:1

EXPERIENCE

Music by Wolfgang Amadeus Mozart

Name: Sts. Priscilla and Aquila
Feast Day: July 8

Priscilla and Aquila were a Jewish couple who lived around the time of Christ. We can read a bit about their lives in Scripture (Acts and Romans). They were originally from Rome but eventually moved to Corinth, and it was there they met St. Paul and welcomed him into their home while he was there spreading the Gospel. They converted to Christianity, and while

Aquila maintained his job as a tent-maker, he and Priscilla dedicated their lives, home and goods to the service of the Church. They even traveled with St. Paul on his missionary journey to Ephesus. In those days, there were no public churches, for Christianity was illegal, so Priscilla and Aquila offered their house in Rome as a "home church" where Christians could gather and Mass could be celebrated. According to tradition, Priscilla and Aquila traveled back to Rome and were martyred there.

Aquila and Priscilla were a courageous couple who spent their lives in service of Christ and his Church. St. Luke mentions them by name in Acts 18, as well as St. Paul in 1 Corinthians 16 and 2 Timothy 4. He had this to say about them in Romans 16:3–5: "Greet Prisca and Aq'uila, my fellow workers in Christ Jesus, who risked their necks for my life, to whom not only I but also all the churches of the Gentiles give thanks; greet also the church in their house." Their love for God gave them the strength to "risk their necks" for the Christian community, and they did it together. They walked with one another toward God, and strove for holiness through their unity with one another. They are remembered in the Roman Martyrology on July 8.

Think of another saint or a hero from your own life. Is there a teacher, family member or friend who reminds you of Sts. Priscilla and Aquila?

Name: _____

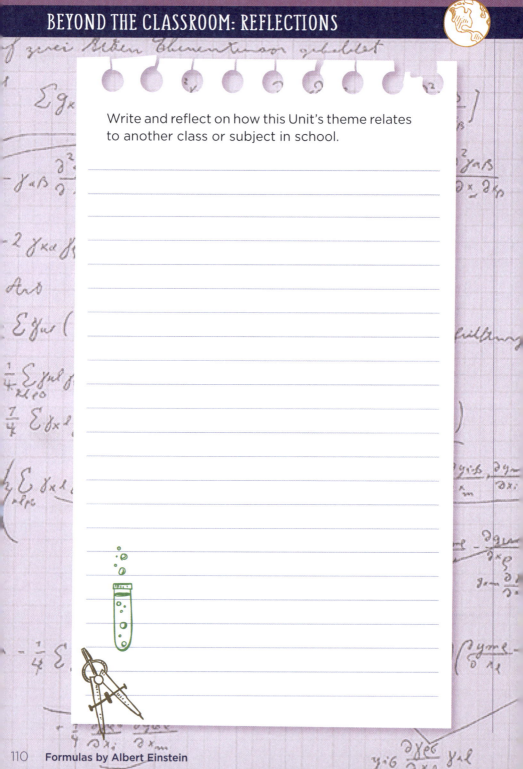

Write and reflect on how this Unit's theme relates to another class or subject in school.

UNIT SIX:

ORIGINAL
nakedness

Sketch by Albrecht Durer (1510)

Reflect on your *lectio divina* time. What is a phrase or image that stands out to you? Write or draw below.

Record a verse to memorize.

"I PRAISE THEE, FOR THOU ART FEARFUL AND WONDERFUL. WONDERFUL ARE THY WORKS! THOU KNOWEST ME RIGHT WELL."

–PSALM 139:14

> ### "THE MAN AND HIS WIFE WERE BOTH NAKED, YET THEY FELT NO SHAME."
>
> Genesis 2:25

THE BODY AS A SIGN

The revelation of the body allows us to discover something extraordinary in what we see as ordinary. We don't often spend much time thinking about the deeper meaning of our bodies when we go about our day, but that meaning is there and informs everything about who we are and what we do. The body as the revelation of the person reminds us of who we are and the greatness to which we are called. I did not create myself, but rather I come from another. This reminds me that I and all of creation are a gift and I am called to make a gift-of-self to others and to the world.

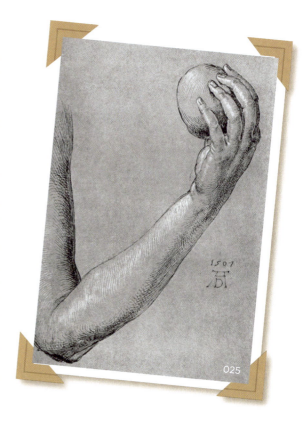

025

Most deeply, as we saw in the experience of original solitude, I am made by God and made to be in relationship with God. Being made in his image and likeness I am called to a special communion with him that is unique and unrepeatable. This communion with God naturally opens itself to a communion with others who are in communion with him. The experience of original unity shows that I come to know more about myself through my relationships with others and that I find myself most fulfilled in making a gift-of-self. It is the body that allows us to see the truth of these original experiences. The body reveals the person: the person who is made in the image and likeness of God and who is given a special dignity over all creation.

ORIGINAL NAKEDNESS

026

The third original experience is called "original nakedness." It is based on the Scripture passage in Genesis that completes the account of the creation of Eve: "The man and his wife were both naked, yet they felt no shame" (Genesis 2:25). Why is this detail so important? And why does it make us feel a bit uncomfortable to hear it read out loud? It can seem like a silly detail that doesn't mean very much, but John Paul II thought it was important to discover what this phrase tells us about the human person, created male and female.

Original nakedness is the original pure vision of the person. It allows Adam and Eve to see one another as they truly are, as expressed in the body. Everything that we have said about the body and its power to reveal the person and express love is immediately obvious to Adam and Eve, simply in the experience of standing before each other. It is the experience of seeing the person as God sees them, and therefore treating him with the reverence that is due. In this experience one is able to fully understand the true value of the whole person. It is the experience of seeing the other more fully and clearly.

> "THE BODY ... REMINDS US OF WHO WE ARE AND THE GREATNESS TO WHICH WE ARE CALLED."

In this way, Adam and Eve could relate to one another freely and without worry of being used, misunderstood or taken for granted. It is a vision that allowed Adam and Eve to see more than the surface level of flesh and bones and to look instead into the deepest truth of who the other person is. They were able to see how the body is a revelation of the person, which includes flesh and bone but is also so much more. This is what allowed for free, true and real communication and communion between the two.

CLEAR AND TRUE VISION

This is perhaps difficult for us to imagine because our own experience isn't the same as that of Adam and Eve. After original sin a dramatic change occurred in our experience of original nakedness: we no longer have the eyes to see the world as Adam and Eve did before original sin. Indeed, every original experience is affected in some way by sin, but perhaps the experience of original nakedness is affected most obviously. Sin fractured that original, whole, true, clear vision of the other person that made it possible for man to see all the glory and dignity of the human person when looking at the body of another. In other words, it is now possible to simply reduce the fullness of who the person is to how he appears in his body. This is also why it can

> "ORIGINAL NAKEDNESS IS THE ORIGINAL, PURE VISION OF THE PERSON."

perhaps be a bit uncomfortable to read the words of Scripture about being naked. In our fallen condition, it takes effort not only to see the body clearly but also to think and talk about it properly, that is, with reverence. Ultimately it can only be done through the grace of God.

The body, which once was an unquestionable sign of the image of God in man, is now at risk of not being seen for what it truly is. After original sin it is not possible to have the fullness of the vision of the person in his nakedness. In fact, now we must cover the body's nakedness in order to help us see the person more clearly. Even though we do not experience original nakedness as Adam and Eve did, this experience challenges us to try and recover as much as possible the true vision of the other person and work to repair the brokenness caused by sin. Original nakedness calls us to rediscover the true meaning of the body and all that it reveals to us.

"WE NO LONGER HAVE THE EYES TO SEE THE WORLD AS ADAM AND EVE DID."

Letter written by St. Teresa of Calcutta

KALOS

Ornamental Page from Greek Gospels (date unknown)

1. What does it mean that the body is a sign, that it reveals the person? What is the body able to show? (You may want to go back to "Unit 3: The Body Reveals Man.")

_____

_____

_____

_____

_____

_____

_____

_____

_____

_____

2. What does "original nakedness" mean? What does it mean for the way Adam and Eve saw one another?

_____

_____

_____

_____

_____

_____

_____

_____

_____

_____

_____

3. Why didn't Adam and Eve feel shame, even though they were unclothed?

4. How did original sin damage the experience of original nakedness? Name at least two consequences.

5. Is there a particular character in a book, movie, or TV show *who was* overlooked, misjudged or gossiped about? How did it impact them and the other characters?

_____

_____

_____

_____

_____

_____

_____

_____

_____

_____

_____

_____

6. Is there a particular character in a book, movie, or TV show that overlooked, misjudged or gossiped about *someone else*? How did it impact them and the other characters?

_____

_____

_____

_____

_____

_____

_____

_____

_____

_____

_____

7. List some ways you can recover a sense of original nakedness: that is, seeing others—and yourself—with the pure and true vision of God and treating them with the reverence that is due.

_____

_____

_____

_____

_____

_____

_____

_____

_____

For personal reflection: Reflect on your own experience: Have *you* ever had the experience of being overlooked, misjudged or seen as something that you aren't? What did you wish the other person saw or understood about you?

_____

_____

_____

For personal reflection: Reflect on your own experience: Have you ever overlooked, misjudged or gossiped about *someone else*? Why did you do so? What were you thinking about the other person (if anything at all)?

_____

_____

_____

"'NAKEDNESS' SIGNIFIES THE ORIGINAL GOOD OF THE DIVINE VISION."
—TOB 13:1

EXPERIENCE

Ornamental Page from Greek Gospels (date unknown)

Name: St. Germaine Cousin
Feast Day: June 15

Germaine was born to poor parents in Pibrac, France in 1579. She suffered from a condition that caused physical deformities, and because of this was not allowed to live in her home. She took care of the family's flock of sheep, watching them day and night, and she slept in the barn with the animals at night. Germaine had a difficult relationship with her stepmother, who often took her for granted and treated her more like a servant than a stepdaughter. But Germaine chose to show patience, humility and gentleness. She had a deep devotion to Jesus in the Eucharist and would attend mass every day. Many of the townspeople often teased

029

her for her deformed and strange-looking body, but the children of the town, to whom she spoke about the love of God, loved her. Eventually her family and the townspeople began to see her joy beneath her illnesses and tried to assist her in her troubles. She died at the age of 22, in the barn, surrounded by the animals.

The life of St. Germaine reminds us all to see others with the eyes of God, and not to judge another based on appearances. No matter the sickness, disability or difficulty, each and every human person is loved immeasurably by God. We are reminded that in a fallen world, the body doesn't always clearly communicate who the person is. As a sign of this, upon her death, Germaine's body was healed of its boils and her skin cleared. In addition, her body remained incorrupt and many miracles began happening when people came to pray by her tomb. Germaine challenges us to not only live joyfully in suffering, but also to keep a pure vision of the other person, and strive to see and love them as God does.

Think of another saint or a hero from your own life. Is there a teacher, family member or friend who reminds you of St. Germaine Cousin?

Name:

Write or draw something memorable from this Unit.

Sketch by Thomas Edison

Analogy: a way of describing the relationship between two things which are similar but also very (and even more) dissimilar.

Communion: a deep union/unity with another. More than a simple interaction with something or someone. For example, you may have interactions with strangers at the supermarket, but communion usually comes with people close to you, like friends.

Communion of persons: when two (or more) persons form a deep unity by giving themselves to one another in love, in order to form a specific kind of unity. This phrase has been used to describe the Trinity, but also the unity of the Church, the family and the unity of man and woman.

Covenant: the special relationship established between God and humanity. This is different from a contract. A contract is a legally binding document that is able to change. The covenant of God and man is a law established out of love in order to help man, and is forever. Before the coming of Christ, it is referred to as the Old Covenant. Jesus fulfilled the Old Covenant and established the New Covenant.

Creator: another name for God.

Creation: everything that is not the Creator (God).

Dominion: the gift of responsibility that man has for all creation.

Embodied soul/living body: ways of speaking about the human person as a whole (to include all that is visible and invisible).

Essential: necessary for a thing to be what it is (example: "It is essential for a triangle to have three sides").

Ex nihilo: a Latin phrase that means "out of/from nothing". It is commonly used to describe the way God creates. When God creates, he doesn't use pre-existing material, he creates ex nihilo, from nothing.

Experience: how I see the world in light of truth; my own way of living and seeing objective reality; objective reality lived by me.

Fundamental/foundational: the most basic and important.

Fundamental relationships: man's most basic and important relationships: to God, self, others and the world. These relationships are connected, and when one is broken, they are all broken; when one is restored, the others are restored.

Gift-of-self: thoughts, words or actions that place myself at the service of others and seek the true good of the other.

Hierarchy: an order that preserves the right relationships of parts in a whole, of persons to each other, or of creatures to the Creator. (For example, there is a hierarchy on a soccer team: a coach, a captain and other players. This order helps keep all the parts working properly as a whole, as a team. Good leadership helps all the players be better and achieve their potential.)

Image of God: the way Scripture talks about the unique dignity of the human person. Male and female are most like God of all creation; they are made in God's image and likeness.

Original experiences: the most basic human experiences; all humanity has these in common. First experienced by Adam and Eve, and also experienced by all of us. Based on the Genesis account, John Paul II names three: original solitude, original unity, original nakedness.

   Original solitude: the experience of man's being alone-with-God; his unique relation to God.

   Original unity: the experience of man's unity-in-difference; the unique relation between male and female.

   Original nakedness: the experience of the true and clear vision of the person.

Original sin/the Fall: the first sin committed by Adam and Eve. They doubted the goodness of God, believed the lie of the serpent and turned away from God. This sin is passed on to every human person (except Mary). We are all born with original sin and need baptism to free us from it.

Revelation: God's special word about himself to mankind.

Reverence: to see things, animals and people the way God does, and treat them with the dignity owed to each; a sacred or holy respect. We reverence something when we honor and respect what it is and treat it accordingly.

LIST OF IMAGES

UNIT 1

001. Jacopo Tintoretto, *Creation of the Animals* (1550)
002. Jan Brueghel the Elder, *The Temptation in the Garden of Eden* (1600)
003. Fra Angelico, *The Crucifixion* (1420–1423)
004. Photo of Bl. Pier Giorgio Frassati, catholicexchange.com

UNIT TWO

005. Raphael, The Creation of the Animals (1519)
006. Flemish School, God Creating the Birds and Animals (17th cent.)
007. Jan Brueghel the Younger, *Creation of Adam in the Paradise* (17th cent.)
008. Andrej Rublev, *Trinity* (1411)
009. Vincent Van Gogh, *First Steps* (after Millet) (1890)
010. Manfredo Ferrari, St. Teresa of Calcutta (1985), commons.wikimedia.org

UNIT THREE

011. Michelangelo, *The Creation of Adam* (1508–1512)
012. Johannes Vermeer, *Girl with a Pearl Earring* (1665)
013. Caravaggio, *Incredulity of Saint Thomas* (1602)
014. Jean-Francois Millet, *L'Angelus* (1857–1859)
015. Photo of Saint Andre Bessette (created before 1938)

UNIT FOUR

016. Hildegard von Bingen, *The Cosmic Spheres and Human Being* (1230)
017. Henri Rousseau, *The Monkeys in the Jungle* (1909)
018. Charles Joseph Natoire, *The Rebuke of Adam and Eve* (1740)
019. Antonio del Pollaiolo, *Assumption of St. Mary* (1460)

UNIT FIVE

020. Ekkehard Ritter, *God Creating Eve* (Basilica di San Marco in Venice), Image Collections and Fieldwork Archives, Dumbarton Oaks, Washington, D.C.
021. English School, *Creation of Eve* (13th cent.)
022. Henri Martin, *Lovers at Spring* (1902)
023. Pieter Bruegel the Elder, *The Wedding Dance* (1566)
024. Engraving of Sts. Priscilla and Aquila (date unknown)

UNIT SIX

025. Albrecht Durer, *Arm of Eve* (1507)
026. Hendrick Goltzius, *The Fall of Man* (1616)
027. Caravaggio, *Narcissus* (1599)
028. *Expulsion from Eden* (Cathedral of the Assumption in Monreale, Sicily, 12th–13th cent.)
029. William-Adolphe Bougeureau, *A Little Shepherdess* (1891)

Trinity: Who God is. One God in three persons: Father, Son and Holy Spirit. We don't believe in three gods. We believe in one God who, within that unity, has a difference of persons. This is a great mystery and was revealed most clearly when Christ (the Son) came into the world and revealed this truth to us.

Unity-in-difference: one reality (unity) that has difference within it (difference). Man and woman are both the same and different, and they are able to be united in a unique way because of their difference.